The delivery truck bounces down the country road.

It has a delivery to make at...

THE POTTERY PLACE

by Gail Gibbons

Harcourt Brace Jovanovich, Publishers
San Diego   New York   London

For Phyllis Eva Murray
of South Road Pottery
in Bradford, Vermont

Library of Congress Cataloging-in-Publication Data
Gibbons, Gail.
The pottery place.
Summary: Describes the history and process of potterymaking by following a potter
through a day of work.
1. Pottery—Juvenile literature. [1. Pottery]
I. Title.
TP808.2.G53 1987   666'.3   86-3279C
ISBN 0-15-263265-4

First edition
A B C D E

The illustrations in this book were done in watercolor on Whatman heavyweight watercolor paper.
The text type was set in Icone Light by Thompson Type, San Diego, California.
The display type was hand-set in Abbey by Thompson Type, San Diego, California.
Printed and bound by Tien Wah Press, Singapore
Production supervision by Warren Wallerstein and Eileen McGlone
Designed by Francesca M. Smith

A woman comes through the gate of the Pottery Place. She is a potter—someone who makes mugs, bowls, and other pottery from clay. Her dry clay has just arrived.

The delivery person and the potter carry the bags inside. The potter uses different kinds of clay for different reasons—for texture or strength, depending on how her pottery will be used. All the many kinds of clay come from the ground.

This morning the potter has time to mix up some new batches of clay. She follows her own recipes. She mixes her dry powder recipe together, then adds it to water until it becomes soft clay.

 Now she leaves it alone. She has other things to do at the Pottery Place. She has some mugs to make, and also a big pot that a neighbor ordered. She takes out soft clay that is about a year old. The older the clay, the better.

She begins to *wedge* the clay, or knead it, to get the air bubbles out. The air bubbles must be removed, so that the pottery won't crack or explode while it is baking.

A friend comes to watch the potter at work. The potter pushes the clay back and forth, back and forth. It becomes smoother and smoother.

"Have some tea," the potter offers, taking a break. The two drink their tea and talk about pottery. The friend asks, "How long have people been making pottery?"

American Indian bowl, about 1,300 years old

American Indian cooking pot, about 1,400 years old

jar from Mexico, about 1,500 years old

urn from Mexico, about 1,500 years old

vessel from Peru, about 1,400 years old

"For thousands and thousands of years," the potter replies.

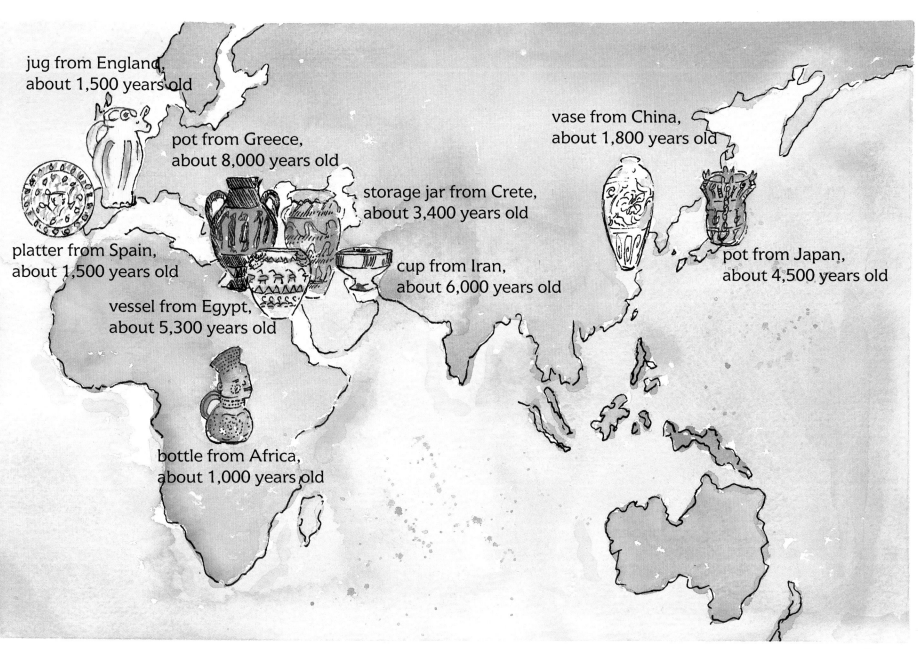

jug from England,
about 1,500 years old

pot from Greece,
about 8,000 years old

vase from China,
about 1,800 years old

storage jar from Crete,
about 3,400 years old

platter from Spain,
about 1,500 years old

cup from Iran,
about 6,000 years old

pot from Japan,
about 4,500 years old

vessel from Egypt,
about 5,300 years old

bottle from Africa,
about 1,000 years old

"Pottery has been found all over the world."

Finally the clay is ready. It is nice and flexible. It has what the potter calls "good body." She wants to make the mugs first. She rolls the clay out and tears off a section for each mug.

wheel head

shaft

flywheel

kick wheel

Now she uses her potter's wheel. She places a lump of clay on the center of the wheel. She dips her hands in a bowl of water. Then she kicks the flywheel to make it spin.

As the kick wheel spins, the potter pushes her wet fingers into the center of the spinning clay. It begins to take on a new shape. Now it has low, thick sides.

modeling tool

inside tool

outside tool

sponge

wire

knife

rib

By working one hand on the inside and the other hand on the outside of the clay, the potter begins to draw up the clay into the shape of a mug. She thinks about how the mug will look and uses her imagination to shape the clay until one mug is finished.

 The potter, with a smooth rhythm, does this over and over . . . until twelve mugs are lined up. She'll add their handles tomorrow.

Next she begins to make the big pot. She places more clay on the wheel, then kicks and kicks. The wheel whirls around again. The pot slowly becomes taller, taller . . . and taller. Then the potter gently separates the pot from the wheel with her wire.

She covers the pieces with a sheet of plastic so they won't dry too quickly.
A man comes into the Pottery Place. He wants the potter to make a teapot and she writes the order down.

kiln

A whole batch of pottery she made last week is dry enough to be *bisqued*, or baked. At this stage the pottery is called *greenware*. She has decorated some with designs painted on in *slip*, which is a creamy, colored clay. She has cut designs into the surface of other pieces. Now the potter carefully places them all into a special oven called a *kiln*.

inside view of kiln

cones

The potter stacks the greenware in tightly. Near a peephole, she places *cones* made of special clay. The heat is turned on to *fire* the pottery.

The temperature goes up and up, very slowly. The potter checks the cones through the peephole from time to time. When the cones start to bend, the potter knows it is time to shut the kiln off.

 The kiln cools. More time goes by. When the kiln is cool enough, the potter carefully removes the fired pottery.

Now she wants to color her pottery. She slowly pours on the glazes . . . but they have no color yet. They will become brilliant colors once they are fired in the kiln.

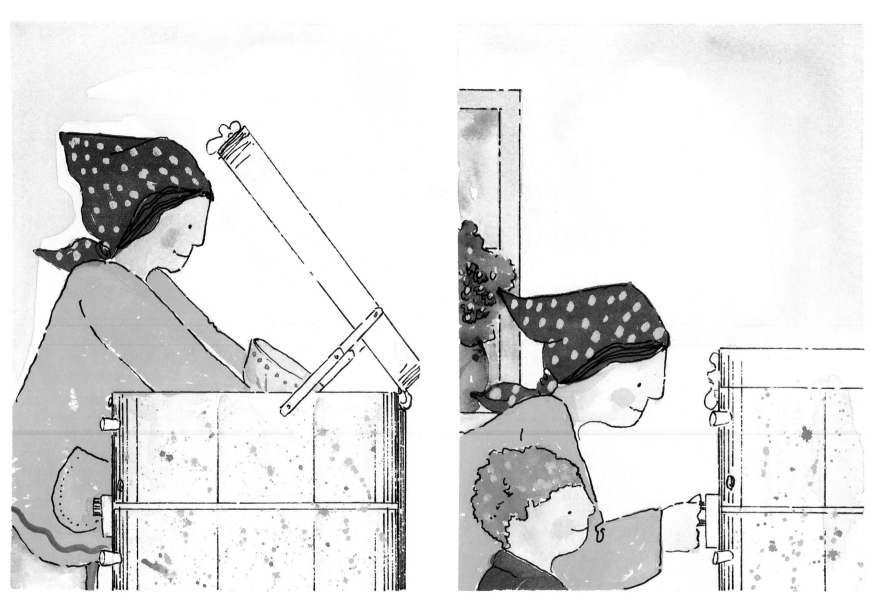

Everything goes into the kiln again. This time the pots cannot touch one another because the glazes will stick together. The temperature climbs, higher this time, to the correct degree for firing the potter's glazes. Then she shuts the kiln off and lets it cool again.

It's time to remove the finished pottery. The pieces are beautiful!

The potter has promised to deliver some of her pottery to a gift shop in town. She carefully wraps the pieces, places them in boxes, and packs them in her van.
The first stop is at a neighbor's house. This vase is for her.

The next stop is the gift shop. The boxes of pottery are carried in and unpacked. The shop owner pays the potter and sets up a display.

The customers admire the wonderful pottery. . .

while the potter drives back to the Pottery Place.

HOW TO MARE YOUR OWN POTTERY

This book describes one traditional method of pottery-making.
Here are three simple methods you can use to make your own pottery.
A kiln is not needed if you use *ready-to-use air-dry clay*.

THE PINCH POT

1. Roll the clay into a ball between your hands.
2. Push your thumbs down into the center of the ball.
3. Pinch the edges to bring up the sides of the pot.
4. When the clay is hardened, decorate the pot with tempera paints.

THE COIL POT

1. Take a piece of the clay and roll it into a ball.
2. Flatten it to make the bottom of the pot.
3. Roll the rest of the clay into long strips.
4. Using the bottom of the pot as the foundation, coil the strips on top of one another.
5. Dip your fingers into a bowl of water and smooth out the coils.
6. When the pot is hard, color it with tempera paints.

THE SLAB POT

1. Use a rolling pin to flatten the clay into a big slab.
2. Cut out five squares the same size from the slab.
3. Use one square slab for the base of the pot.
4. Then carefully place the other four square slabs at right angles to the base to form the sides of the pot.
5. Dip your fingers into a bowl of water and smooth out the seams.
6. When the pot hardens, decorate the pot with tempera paints.